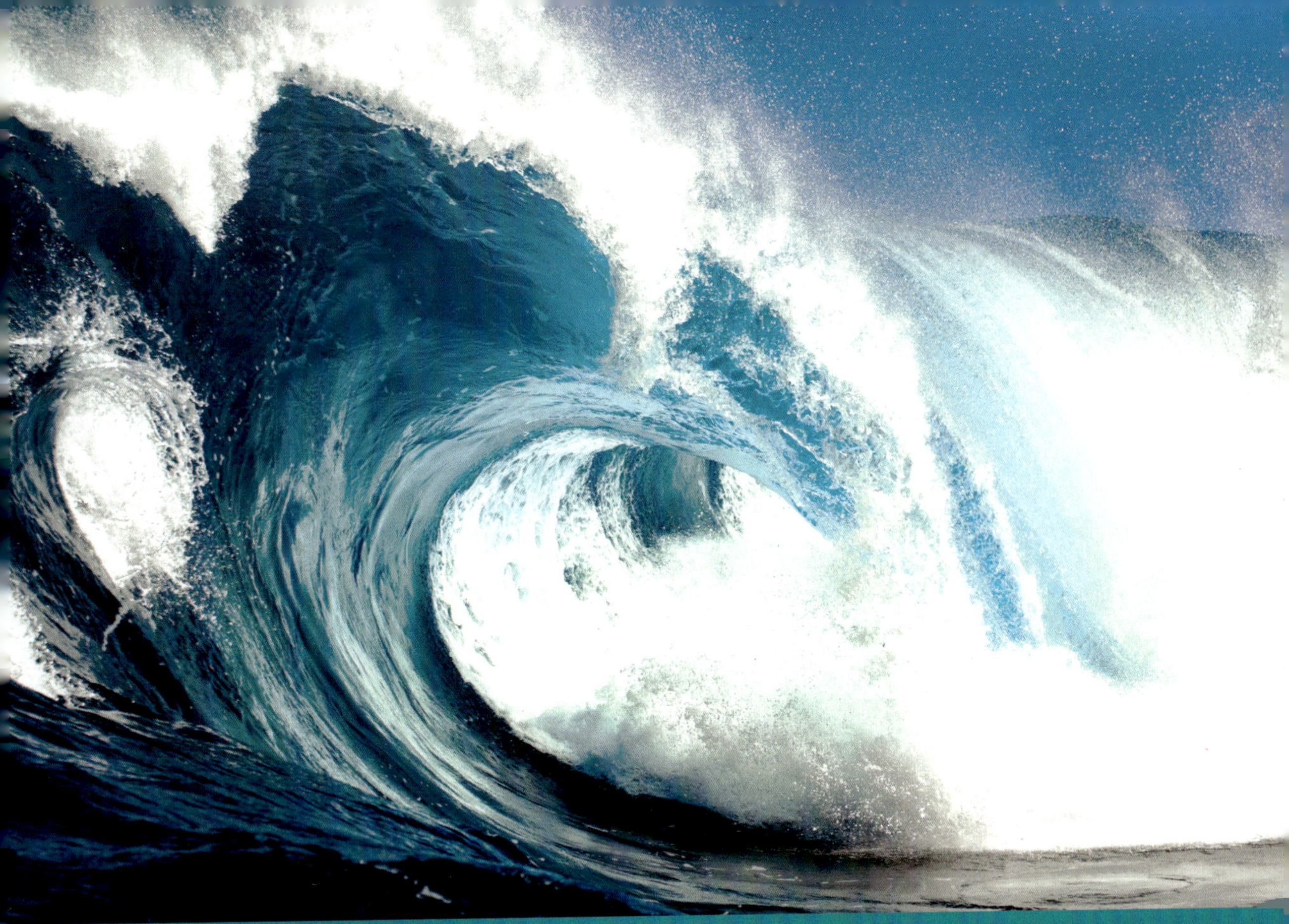

Natural Resources

WATER

Jason McClure and John Willis

LIGHTBOX
openlightbox.com

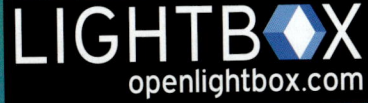

Go to
www.openlightbox.com
and enter this book's
unique code.

ACCESS CODE

LBL46364

Lightbox is an all-inclusive digital solution for the teaching and learning of curriculum topics in an original, groundbreaking way. Lightbox is based on National Curriculum Standards.

STANDARD FEATURES OF LIGHTBOX

 **AUDIO** High-quality narration using text-to-speech system

 ACTIVITIES Printable PDFs that can be emailed and graded

 SLIDESHOWS Pictorial overviews of key concepts

 VIDEOS Embedded high-definition video clips

 WEBLINKS Curated links to external, child-safe resources

 TRANSPARENCIES Step-by-step layering of maps, diagrams, charts, and timelines

 INTERACTIVE MAPS Interactive maps and aerial satellite imagery

 QUIZZES Ten multiple choice questions that are automatically graded and emailed for teacher assessment

 KEY WORDS Matching key concepts to their definitions

Copyright © 2017 Smartbook Media Inc. All rights reserved.

Natural Resources

CONTENTS

- 2   Lightbox Access Code
- 4   Water Resources
- 5   Fresh Water
- 6   Water in the United States
- 8   Water Processing
- 9   The Water Industry
- 10   Using Water
- 12   Water in Industry
- 13   Water in Food
- 14   Dams
- 15   Hydroelectricity
- 16   Making Drinkable Water
- 18   Managing Water
- 20   Water Industry Jobs
- 21   Quiz
- 22   Activity
- 23   Key Words/Index
- 24   Log on to www.openlightbox.com

Water Resources

Water is one of the most important resources on Earth. Water covers 70 percent of Earth's surface. Most of this water is found in the world's oceans. Ocean water is salt water, which is salty and undrinkable.

People need fresh water to survive. Only about 2.5 percent of the water on Earth is fresh water and only 0.007 percent of the water can be used by people. This is because about 99 percent of all fresh water is deep underground or trapped in ice, such as glaciers. The fresh water supply that is trapped deep underground is called **nonrenewable** water.

World Water Supply

The world's water supply is divided into fresh water and salt water. Most of the world's water is salt water found in oceans and seas.

97.5%
Salt water
(Ocean and seas)

2.5%
Fresh water
(Lakes, rivers, and groundwater)

Natural Resources

In total, Earth contains about 332 million cubic miles (1.4 billion cubic kilometers) of water.

Fresh Water

Renewable fresh water is water that falls as rain or snow. This water, called **precipitation**, keeps rivers filled. People rely on renewable fresh water for drinking and other uses. However, there are more than 7 billion people in the world. Some scientists think the population will pass 9 billion by 2050. All of these people need water, but the amount of fresh water is not changing. As the world's population continues to grow, so will the value of water.

2.5 million cubic miles
(10.5 million km³)
Volume of fresh groundwater in the world

763 cubic miles
(3,069 km³)
Volume of fresh water in the United States

4 cubic miles
(17.7 km³)
Volume of daily precipitation in the lower 48 states

Water 5

Water in the United States

The United States holds about 8 percent of the world's fresh water. The water supply of the United States is renewed by precipitation. However, this precipitation is not spread equally across the country. Dry areas, such as the desert in Nevada, get very little rainfall each year. Other states, such as Florida and Louisiana, get plenty of yearly precipitation. Another important source of water is groundwater. Groundwater is water that flows below the ground. This water can be accessed by digging wells. About 50 percent of Americans get their water from groundwater sources.

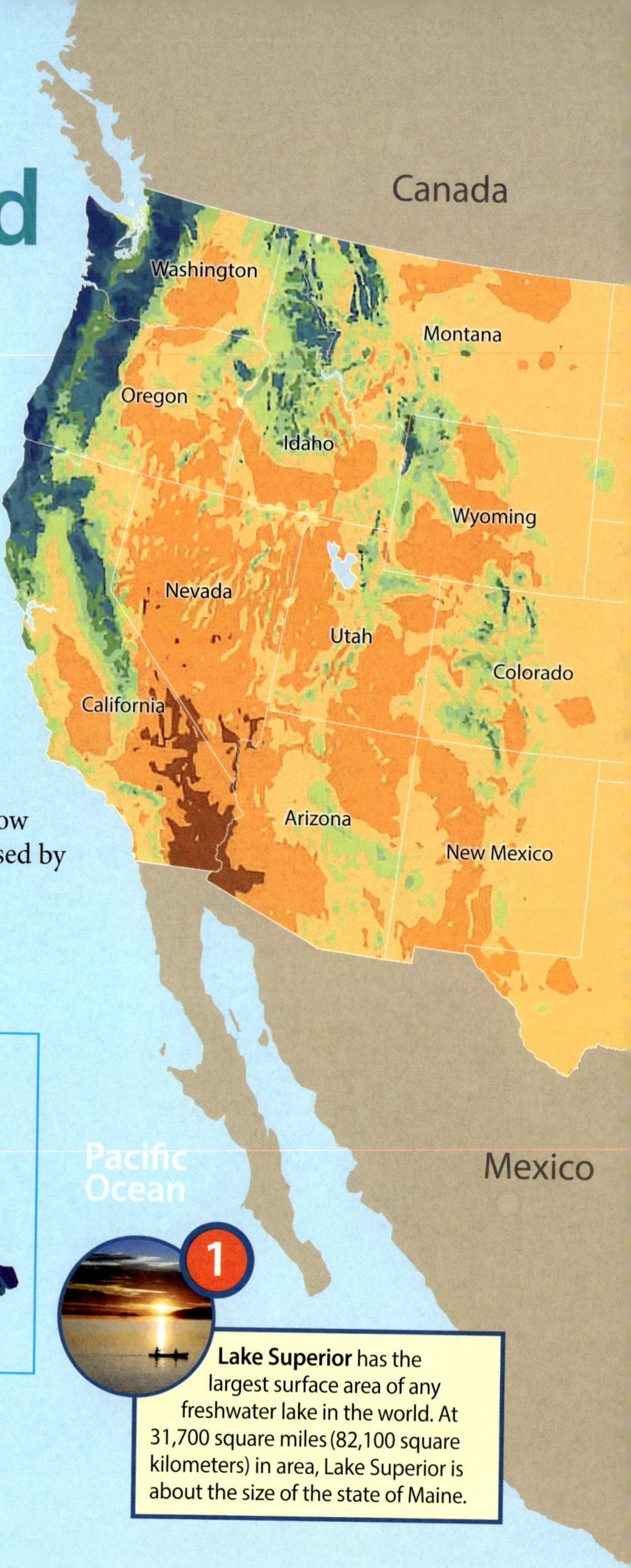

1 Lake Superior has the largest surface area of any freshwater lake in the world. At 31,700 square miles (82,100 square kilometers) in area, Lake Superior is about the size of the state of Maine.

6   Natural Resources

Water 7

The average American pays about 25 cents each day for the water he or she uses.

Water Processing

Whether it comes from lakes, rivers, reservoirs, or the ground, water needs to be cleaned before it can be brought to people's homes and businesses. Water is pumped from a source—a river or lake—to a water treatment plant. At the plant, water is sent through filters, which remove dirt and any other objects. Chemicals are also added to the water to help kill germs that can pass through the filters. The clean water is then pumped to homes and businesses. Once it has been used, the water goes through pipes to a waste treatment plant. Here, the water is cleaned again before being returned to the river or lake.

How Americans Get Water

Before it can be used by Americans, water from rivers or lakes must be cleaned at a treatment plant. After the water is used, it goes back to another treatment facility to be cleaned before it is pumped back into lakes and rivers to begin the cycle anew.

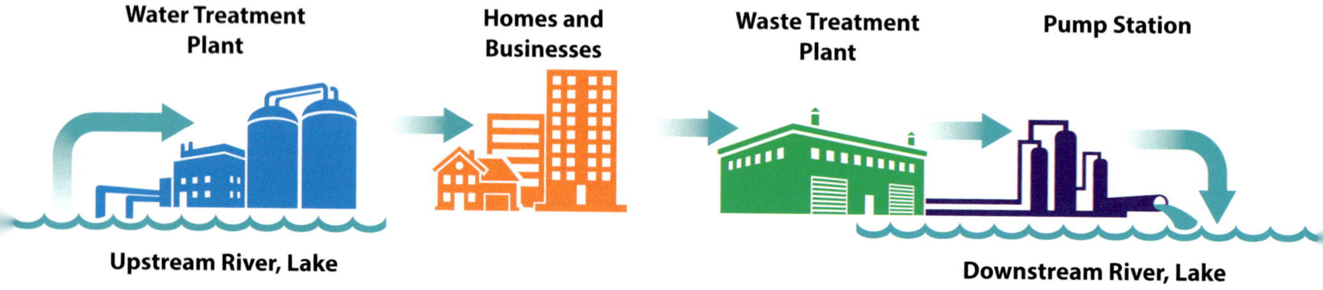

Water Treatment Plant
Upstream River, Lake

Homes and Businesses

Waste Treatment Plant   **Pump Station**
Downstream River, Lake

8   Natural Resources

The Water Industry

Water is an industry itself. In the United States, the water treatment industry is worth almost $17 billion. The water industry does important work. It helps cities and towns in the United States provide clean water for their citizens. Some companies make filters that help make dirty water into clean water.

Bottled water is a growing industry in the United States. Americans drank 11 billion gallons (41.6 billion L) of bottled water in 2014, making the United States the tenth-largest consumer of bottled water in the world. Much of this water comes from sources inside the United States.

Bottled water will be the most consumed beverage in the United States in 2017.

10 billion gallons
Amount of bottled water purchased in the United States each year. (37.8 billion L)

31.8 gallons
The average American buys nearly enough bottled water each year to fill a bathtub. (120 L)

$12.3 billion
Money earned by U.S. bottled water sales in 2013.

Irrigation uses 115 billion gallons (453 billion L) of water every day in the United States.

Using Water

Once water has been cleaned, it can then be used by businesses and individuals. Part of the water supply in the United States is used by people in their homes. A larger portion of the supply is used by different industries and businesses.

Most of the water used for irrigation is used by western states, where there are fewer sources of fresh water. Most of the **thermoelectric power** generation is in eastern states.

U.S. Water Use

Water is used in every home and industry in the United States.

Thermoelectric Power
Fossil fuels, such as coal or oil, are burned to boil water. Steam from the boiling water moves turbines that generate electricity.

44%

Irrigation
Water is evenly distributed to crops, simulating ideal precipitation. This helps plants to grow more consistently.

31%

Residential
Governments and other organizations make clean, drinkable water available to homes.

13%

Industrial
Factories use water for heating, cooling, and cleaning. Water is also necessary for the creation of a variety of products, especially food.

7%

Commercial
In stores and restaurants, water is served to customers, used to make food and drinks, and used for cleaning.

3%

Water 11

Water in Industry

Industry mainly uses water for heating, cooling, and processing. Water is used to cool hot objects such as steel that has been melted down. It is also used to cool the machines that were used to heat the steel. Heating water causes it to boil, which produces steam. Steam can be used for heating objects, moving turbines, or cleaning. During the general manufacturing process, water is used to clean machines, floors, and other surfaces in factories. It is also used to make the final product.

It takes approximately 65 gallons (246 L) of water to produce 5 gallons (18.9 L) of gasoline.

For example, water is used in almost every step of the process of making a car. Water is needed to cool down the steel and machines that are used to make the car. Each part that goes into a car also needs to be washed before it can be used. Water itself is used to make the car's tires. In total, it takes about 31,700 gallons (120,000 L) of water to produce one vehicle. This is equal to 271 bathtubs full of water.

The United States manufactures 12.1 million automobiles per year.

12 Natural Resources

Water in Food

Water is used to make food. In fact, it can take hundreds of gallons of water to make some foods. There are many steps in making food, and each one needs water. For example, a large amount of water goes into making a hamburger. Water is used to grow the grain the cattle eat. Every day, the cattle also need to drink water. Later, water is used to clean the beef when it is made into hamburger. It is also used to clean the machines that make the hamburger, which helps keep germs out of the food.

Of all the fresh water on Earth, 27 percent is used in animal production.

Making Food
This chart shows how much water goes into creating different kinds of food. Each bathtub represents 117 gallons (443 L).

One Chocolate bar — 4 Bathtubs of water

One Bag of Chips — 0.4 Bathtubs of water

One Apple — 0.15 Bathtubs of water

One Hamburger — 5.5 Bathtubs of water

At 770 feet (234.7 meters) tall, the Oroville Dam in California is the tallest dam in the United States.

Dams

The amount of renewable water in the United States changes all the time. Rainfall and water levels never remain the same. This means that the supply of water also changes. One way people try to control the water supply is with dams. Dams are large walls that are built to hold back the water in a river or other waterway. This makes a large lake behind the wall, called a reservoir.

Dams create a large supply of water. This water can be released when it is needed most, such as when there is a drought. The water can also be sent to places that need water, such as farming areas that need water for crops. There are more than 87,000 large dams in the United States. Large dams are typically more than 25 feet (7.6 m) tall and may be built for a variety of purposes, including **hydropower**.

Hydroelectricity

Water is an important source of energy for the United States. Between 6 and 7 percent of the electricity that the United States makes is from hydropower. Hydropower uses the flow of water through dams to create electricity. These dams have large turbines, which are similar to the propellers on a plane. When water flows through the dams, it spins the turbines. The spinning turbines then cause generators to spin. Generators are machines that make electricity.

Some hydroelectric facilities in the United States have been operating for more than 100 years.

Hydroelectricity Around the World

Electricity is measured in terawatts (TW). One terawatt is equal to 1 trillion watts. The average laptop only uses about 15 to 60 watts. The United States produces 259 terawatts of hydroelectricity each year. It is the fourth-largest producer of hydroelectricity in the world.

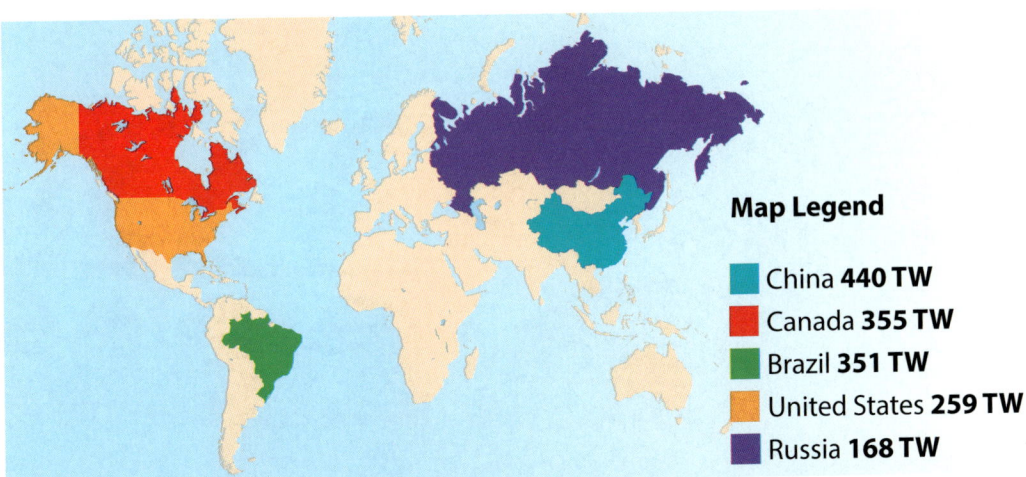

Map Legend

- China **440 TW**
- Canada **355 TW**
- Brazil **351 TW**
- United States **259 TW**
- Russia **168 TW**

Making Water Drinkable

Dirty water causes sickness and death in many parts of the world. Bacteria and other germs can live in water. If a person drinks water that has germs in it, he or she can become very ill. Some diseases that people get from water can be fatal. Each year, diseases from water, such as **cholera**, kill about 3.4 million people around the world. Most of these people live in poor countries that cannot afford to clean their water.

Water Technology Throughout History

Water is the most important substance on Earth. Without water, food would not grow. In fact, humans cannot survive without water for more than a few days. Our first cities were built near water. Early technology was made to carry it. Humans will always depend on water, and the future of water depends on humans.

10,000 BC
Hunter-gatherer groups begin to settle near bodies of water. These early civilizations allow humans to stop migrating.

6000 BC
Irrigation of crops begins in Egypt and Mesopotamia. This watery region is known as the Fertile Crescent because crops grow so well there. In Egypt, the Nile River flooded every year. Farmers used these floods to grow crops. The name Mesopotamia means "between two rivers."

312 BC
Rome begins building a system of **aqueducts**. These stone structures carried water hundreds of miles from the melting ice in the mountains into cities that needed sources of fresh water to grow.

Natural Resources

The chemical chlorine was once very popular for cleaning water, but is becoming less popular due to its negative impacts on the environment. Today, water-cleaning companies in the United States use **ultraviolet**, or UV, light and filtration. UV light is the same light that comes from the Sun. This light can kill bugs and diseases that may be in dirty water.

Filters allow water to pass through, but stop germs and chemicals from going through. The newest water-cleaning technology is **microfiltration**. Microfiltration uses filters with very small holes. In fact, the holes are so small, even the tiniest germ cannot get through. Only water can get through. This method allows water to be cleaned without chemicals.

1800 AD

European countries colonize fertile regions in warmer parts of the world. Irrigated farmland worldwide reaches 19,760,000 acres (8 million hectares).

1969

The Cuyahoga River in Cleveland, Ohio catches fire because of pollution. Anger over the event causes many Americans to push for protection of water and the environment.

1972

The Clean Water Act becomes law, protecting U.S. waterways from pollution. The victory is hard won. Congress has to overturn a veto of the law by President Nixon.

2015

In January 2015, people in Flint, Michigan begin complaining that their tap water tastes funny. Tests show that the water has too much **lead** in it. Lead can damage the brains of children. The crisis brings attention to the problem of lead pipes that carry water into U.S. homes.

Water 17

By the year 2060, Texas plans to produce 10 percent of its new water supplies through recycled waste water.

Managing Water

Water is used by every living organism. In the United States, water supports thousands of species of animals. It helps forests grow, and gives many living things, such as fish, a place to live.

Since water is such an important resource, people, governments, and companies must be very careful about how they use it. These individuals and groups work together to make sure that water resources in the United States are used properly. They also make sure the environment is affected as little as possible.

Governments
Governments set rules that guide how water can be used. These rules state the amount of water that can be used each day. They also tell what must be done to clean any dirty water before it is sent back into rivers and lakes. Some bodies of water are protected by the government from industrial use.

Individuals
Individuals can have an effect on the amount of water they use in their homes. People can collect water from showers or washing machines and use this water, called graywater, to water their lawns. Some people buy water efficient appliances that use less water. They also may report any pollution they find in water sources to the government.

Companies
Companies hire environmental experts to learn about better ways to use water. They sometimes invest millions of dollars to find ways to use less water. Companies also look for new water-saving technologies.

Environmental Groups
Environmental groups work with governments and companies to make sure that companies are following the rules and using water correctly. These groups are also involved in protecting important water sources. The work of environmental groups can help protect U.S. water resources.

Water 19

Water Industry Jobs

There is a wide range of jobs within the water industry. Each job has different tasks to perform and requires a certain type of training.

Hydrologist

Duties: Study water and the environment

Education: University degree in science or engineering

Hydrologists study how water affects people and how people affect water. They study how new buildings may affect nearby water supplies. Some hydrologists try to show farmers better ways to use the water to help them grow more crops.

Plumber

Duties: Build and fix water systems in buildings

Education: College certification and on-the-job training

Plumbers make sure the water supply is safe and clean for houses and businesses. They build the systems that move clean water to where it can be used. They also build the systems that move used, dirty water to sewers and water treatment plants.

Engineer

Duties: Creating water technology

Education: College or university degree

Engineers plan, design, build, and analyze tools and machines for collecting, storing, cleaning, and delivering water. They research and create new processes, systems, and equipment to be used by industries and governments.

20 Natural Resources

Quiz

1. What country is the top producer of hydroelectricity?
2. How many large dams are in the United States?
3. In what part of the world is the Fertile Crescent?
4. What percentage of electricity in the United States is produced by hydropower?
5. How much bottled water did Americans drink in 2014?
6. What percentage of Earth's water is fresh water?
7. What percentage of the world is covered in water?
8. What percentage of Americans get their water from groundwater sources?
9. When did irrigation first begin?
10. In which year did the Clean Water Act become law?

ANSWERS
1 China 2 About 87,000 3 Egypt and Mesopotamia 4 Between 6 and 7 percent 5 11 billion gallons (42 billion L) 6 About 2.5 percent 7 About 70 percent 8 About 50 percent 9 Around 6,000 BC 10 1972

Water 21

Activity

Make Your Own Water Filter

Materials Needed

Water is often dirty and needs to be cleaned before it can be used. In this activity, you will make your own water filter.

1. Turn the top half of the bottle upside-down and place it inside the bottom half. The top of the bottle will be where the filter goes. The bottom half will hold the filtered water.
2. Place a folded paper towel in the top half of the bottle. Layer the gravel, small pebbles, sand, and cotton balls on top of the paper towel. Put the sand in first, then the small pebbles, gravel, and cotton balls.
3. Make your dirty water by mixing the water, cooking oil, dirt, food coloring, and paper confetti.
4. Pour the dirty water through the filter. Record your findings. Is the filtered water clean? Experiment with different ways of layering the filter, and record your results. Then, try different filter materials, such as a sponge or cloth, and record any differences in your results. Which filters work best? Why do you think that might be?

Key Words

aqueducts: ancient structures that carry water for hundreds of miles into cities

cholera: an illness caused by bacteria in water

fossil fuels: energy sources that formed from the remains of plants and animals that lived long ago

hydropower: energy that is created by the flow of water

lead: a silver-colored metal used in batteries that is poisonous to humans

microfiltration: a type of filtration that removes tiny particles, germs, and other objects from fluids

nonrenewable: a resource that cannot be replaced once it is used

precipitation: water in the form of rain or snow that falls to the ground

thermoelectric power: electricity generated by steam-driven turbines

ultraviolet: a type of radiation invisible to the human eye

Index

China 15, 21
dam 14, 15, 21
drinking 4, 5, 11, 13, 16, 17, 21
fresh water 4, 5, 6, 10, 13, 16, 21
filter 7, 8, 9, 17, 22
food 11, 13, 16
governments 11, 18, 19, 20
groundwater 4, 5, 6, 21
grow 5, 11, 13, 16, 18, 20

hydroelectricity 15, 21
ice 4, 16
industry 9, 11, 12, 20
rivers 4, 5, 7, 8, 14, 16, 17, 19
salt water 4, 6
thermoelectric power 10, 11

LIGHTBOX

➕ SUPPLEMENTARY RESOURCES

Click on the plus icon ➕ found in the bottom left corner of each spread to open additional teacher resources.

- Download and print the book's quizzes and activities
- Access curriculum correlations
- Explore additional web applications that enhance the Lightbox experience

LIGHTBOX DIGITAL TITLES
Packed full of integrated media

VIDEOS

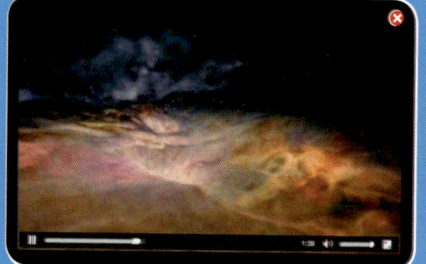

INTERACTIVE MAPS

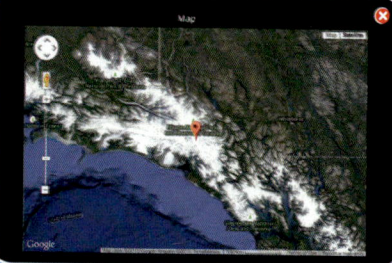

WEBLINKS

SLIDESHOWS

QUIZZES

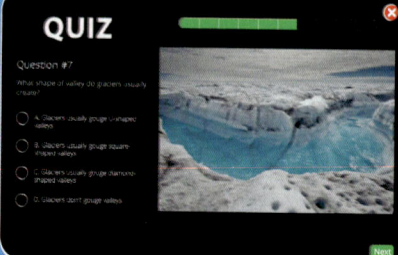

OPTIMIZED FOR
- ✓ **TABLETS**
- ✓ **WHITEBOARDS**
- ✓ **COMPUTERS**
- ✓ **AND MUCH MORE!**

Published by Smartbook Media Inc.
350 5th Avenue, 59th Floor New York, NY 10118
Website: www.openlightbox.com

Copyright © 2017 Smartbook Media Inc.
All rights reserved. No part of this publication may be reproduced, stored in a retrieval system, or transmitted in any form or by any means, electronic, mechanical, photocopying, recording, or otherwise, without the prior written permission of the publisher.

Library of Congress Control Number: 2016931227

ISBN 978-1-5105-1058-6 (hardcover)
ISBN 978-1-5105-1059-3 (multi-user eBook)

Printed in Brainerd, Minnesota, United States
1 2 3 4 5 6 7 8 9 0   20 19 18 17 16

052016
052016

Project Coordinator: Jared Siemens
Art Director: Terry Paulhus

Every reasonable effort has been made to trace ownership and to obtain permission to reprint copyright material. The publisher would be pleased to have any errors or omissions brought to its attention so that they may be corrected in subsequent printings.

The publisher acknowledges Getty Images, iStock, Shutterstock, and Corbis Images as its primary image suppliers for this title.

24 Natural Resources